THE ENGLISH
ANTHEM
COLLECTION

VOLUME TWO

■

Twenty-two anthems
for upper voices,
written between
1960 and 1994

EDITED BY

Helen Burrows

Copyright Information and Acknowledgements

Contents

Unaccompanied anthems are marked*.

Index of Composers

Seasonable Suggestions

Many of these anthems are also suitable for general use.   Unaccompanied anthems are marked*

	Anthem	Composer	No.	Page
Advent/Christmastide	Jesus Christ the apple tree	Holman	12	53
	Mater Ora Filium	Oxley	15	68
	What songs are these?	Lloyd	22	98
Passiontide	Ave verum corpus	Wills	3	16
Easter and Holy Week	An Easter Greeting	How	4	19
	My song is love unknown	Archer	16	74
	Love is come again*	Tamblyn	3	57
Pentecost	The Father's Love	Lole	5	23
	I give you a new commandment	Aston	9	40
Remembrance	For the fallen	Blatchly	7	30
	In Paradisum	Willcocks	11	49
Feasts of Our Lady	Angelus	Mathias	1	6
	Ave Maria	Lindley	2	14
Other Feast Days	Ave verum corpus	Wills	3	16
Communion	Ave verum corpus	Wills	3	16
	O sacrum convivium	Leighton	19	83
Weddings	The Father's Love	Lole	5	23
	A Gaelic Blessing	Rutter	8	37
	I give you a new commandment	Aston	9	41
	I will lift up mine eyes	Mawby	10	45
Baptisms	The Father's Love	Lole	5	23
	A Gaelic Blessing	Rutter	8	37
	I give you a new commandment	Aston	9	41
	Make me a light	Wilby	14	65
Funerals/Memorial	For the fallen	Blatchly	7	30
	I will lift up mine eyes	Mawby	10	45
	In Paradisum	Willcocks	11	49
Festivals	O Sing unto the Lord	Rawsthorne	20	90
	Fill thou my life	Witchell	6	27
General	O for a closer walk with God	Cæsar	17	77
	O hear us, Lord	Piccolo	18	80
	A Song of St Francis*	Hurd	21	92

Preface

The volumes of *The English Anthem Collection* draw together selected church-music compositions of the last half century. The present volume contains twenty-two anthems for upper voices.

The chosen anthems are suitable for use by children's and women's choirs. Many of their accompaniments are possible on a piano or an organ. Two are unaccompanied. A number of them can be used by choirs requiring upper-and-lower-voice music (for example, sopranos and men) in less than four parts.

The RSCM is producing this series as a resource for choirs wishing to broaden their repertoires. But I believe that this initiative is also a tribute to those who, by the high quality of their compositions, are helping to sustain what is the envy of the world, the English choral tradition.

In editing this volume I have had generous support from composers and other musicians and I am very grateful to them all – but particularly to Peter Aston, for his unfailing encouragement and enthusiasm, and to Augusta Miller, whose advice was greatly appreciated during the preliminary stages of selection and preparation.

Helen Burrows
Addington Palace 1995

Commissioned (in association with the Welsh Arts Council)
by the Sirenian Singers

1. Angelus

Words: from the *Angelus*

Music: William Mathias

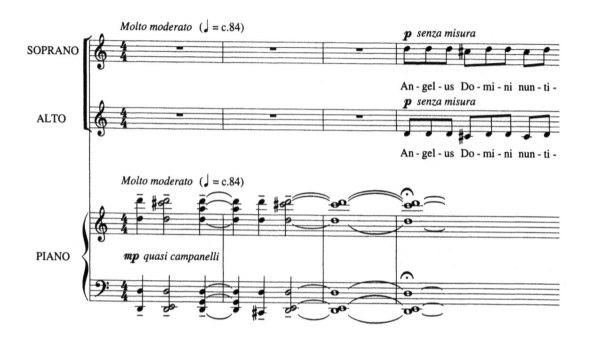

The Angel of the Lord announced unto Mary. And she conceived of the Holy Ghost.

Hail, Mary, full of grace, the Lord is with thee; blessed art thou amongst women, and blessed is the fruit of thy womb, Jesus.

Behold the handmaid of the Lord. Be it done to me according to your word. Hail, Mary, full of grace, ...

And the word was made flesh. And dwelt among us. Hail, Mary, full of grace, ...

ple - na, Do - mi - nus te - cum,____ be - ne - dic - ta tu___ in

ple - na, Do - mi - nus te - cum,____ be - ne - dic - ta tu___ in

mu - li - e - ri - bus,____ et be - ne - dic - tus fruc - tus ven - tris

mu - li - e - ri - bus,____ et be - ne - dic - tus fruc - tus ven - tris

tu - i, Je - sus, Je - sus, Je - sus.

tu - i, Je - sus, Je - sus, Je - sus.

Pray for us, O holy Mother of God.

That we may be made worthy of the promises of Christ. Amen.

9 September 1983

13

2. Ave Maria

Words: from the *Angelus*

Music: Simon Lindley

For the Choristers of Ely Cathedral

3. Ave Verum Corpus

Words: Fourteenth-century hymn, sometimes attributed to Pope Innocent VI (d.1342)　　　　Music: Arthur Wills

O Je - su fi - li Ma - ri - ae, mi - se - re - re

O Je - su fi - li Ma - ri - ae,

me - i, A - men, A -

mi - se - re - re me - i, A - men,

- men, A - men, A - men.

A - men, A - men.

4. An Easter Greeting

Words: Mrs. C.F. Alexander (adapted)

Music: Martin How

Death is con-quered, man is free, Christ is ris-en, Christ is ris-en,

Christ has won the vic-to-ry. For as in

Ad-am all die,___ Ev-en so in Christ shall all be made a-

- live:___ I know___

that my Re - deem - er liv - eth.

(Small Group) Full rit.

The Lord is ris - en, The Lord is ris - en, in - deed.

marcato

Gt. *mf*

Sw. *mp* *marcato*

Sw. Gt. *f* rit.

Ped.

Tempo I, e maestoso

Christ is ris - en, Christ is ris - en, Tell it with a cheer - ful voice,

Tempo I, e maestoso

Christ is ris - en, Christ is ris - en, Let the whole wide earth re - joice.

Al - le - lu - ia, al - le - lu - ia, Death is con - quered, Man is free,

Descant

Largamente

Al - - le - lu - ia, al - - le - lu -

Unison voices

Christ is ris - en, Christ is ris - en, Christ has won the vic - to - ry.

Largamente

(Opt.) *rit.*

A - - men, A - - men.

rit.

Al - le - lu - ia, A - men, A - - men.

rit.

Ped.

For Elizabeth Dodd

5. The Father's Love

Words: John 15; 19–22

Music: Simon Lole

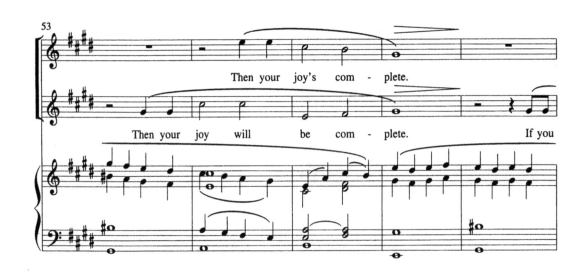

Then your joy's com - plete.

Then your joy will be com - plete. If you

dolce e ardente

dim.

Ah _____ And your joy will

keep__ my com - mand - ments, and you love one a - no - ther, your joy will

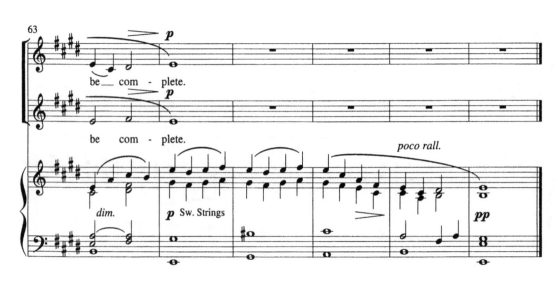

p

be __ com - plete.

be com - plete.

poco rall.

dim.

p Sw. Strings

pp

For Augusta Miller and the
Choir of Sherborne School for Girls

6. Introit: Fill Thou My Life

Words: H. Bonar

Music: Peter J. Witchell

Fill thou my life O Lord my

Fill thou my life O Lord my

God, In ev - ery part with praise,____ That my whole be - ing

God,_ In ev - ery part with praise, That my whole be - ing

may pro - claim thy be - ing and thy ways._____ So shall no part

may pro - claim thy be - ing and thy ways._____ So shall no part_

Day or Night, From sa - cred - ness be free_____ But all my life in

Day or Night, From sa - cred - ness be free__ But all my life_ in

ev - ery step, Be fel - low - ship with thee. A - -

ev - ery step, Be fel - low - ship with thee. A - men,

dim. -

- men, A - men, A - men, A - - men, A - men.

A - men, A - men, A - men, A - men, A - men.

Written for performance at the British Legion Festival of Remembrance at the Royal Albert Hall on 8 November 1980.
For Barry Rose and the Choristers of St. Paul's Cathedral, London.

7. For the Fallen

Words: Lawrence Binyon

Music: Mark Blatchly

With proud thanks-gi-ving, a mo-ther for her chil-dren, Eng - land

mourns for her dead a-cross the sea. Flesh of her flesh they were, Spi - rit___ of__ her__

limb, true of— eye; Stea - dy and a - glow. They were staunch to the end a - gainst

limb, true of eye; Stea - dy and a - glow. They were staunch to the end a - gainst

limb, true of eye; Stea - dy and a - glow. They were staunch to the end a - gainst

odds; Un - count - ed, They fell with their fa - ces to the foe.

They min-gle not with their laugh-ing com-rades a - gain; they sit no
more at fam-il-iar ta-bles at home, They have no lot in our la-bour of the
day-time, They sleep be-yond Eng-land's foam.

They min-gle not with their laugh-ing com-rades a - gain; they sit no
more at fam-il-iar ta-bles at home, They sleep, they sleep, they sleep
be-yond Eng-land's foam.

They shall grow not old,_____ as we that are left___ grow old:____ Age shall not wea - ry them nor the years con - demn. At the go - ing down of the sun and in the

When there is no trumpeter available to take the solo part, it will be found necessary to enlist the aid of a second organist to perform this piece satisfactorily.

Oxford, 10–20 October 1980.

8. A Gaelic Blessing

Words: adapted from an old Gaelic rune

Music: John Rutter

Deep peace___ of the qui-et earth to you,___ Deep peace.

Deep___ peace of the earth to you,___ Deep,___ deep___

Deep___ peace of the earth to you, Deep,___ deep___

___ of the shining stars___ to you, Hum___

peace of the stars to you, Hum___

peace of the stars___ to you,___ Deep peace___ of the gen-tle

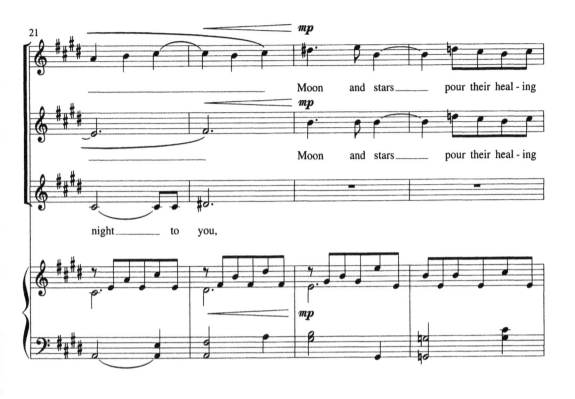

of____ Christ_____ the___ light_____ of the

of____ Christ_____ the__ light_____ of the

of____ Christ_____ the__ light_____ of the

world to you, Deep peace__ of Christ to you.

world to you,____ Deep peace__ of Christ to you.

world to you, Deep peace__ of Christ to___ you.

9. I Give You a New Commandment

Words: John 14, 34–35

Music: Peter Aston

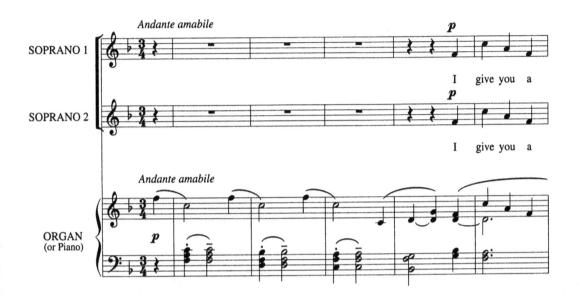

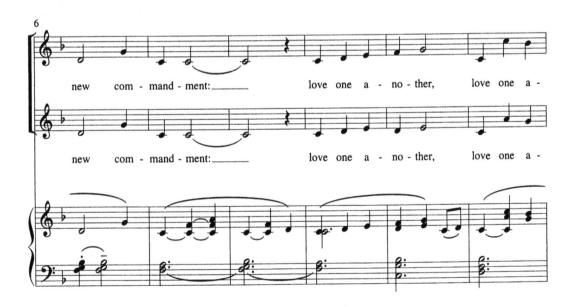

For Lucy and Paul

10. I Will Lift up Mine Eyes

Words: from Psalm 121

Music: Colin Mawby

made hea - ven and earth.____ He will not suf - fer thy foot to be

Man.

mov - ed: he that keep - eth thee will not slum - ber. Be - hold, he that keep - eth__

Ped.

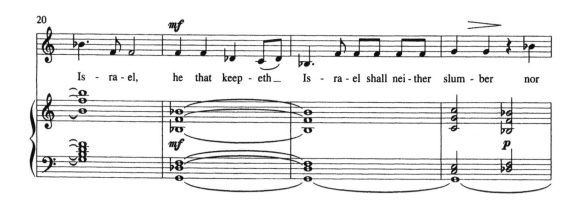

Is - ra - el, he that keep - eth_ Is - ra - el shall nei - ther slum - ber nor

sleep,____ nei - ther slum - ber nor sleep.____ The

Man.

Lord is thy keep-er: The Lord is thy shade up-on thy right hand. The

sun_____ shall not smite thee by day, nor the moon_____ by

Ped.

night. The Lord_____ shall pre-serve thee from all

p very serene

e-vil: he shall pre-serve_____ thy soul.

In loving memory of Patrick MacNamara

11. In Paradisum

Words: from the Burial Service

Music: Jonathan Willcocks

In pa - ra - di - sum de - du - cant
May ho - ly an - gels lead you to

an - ge - li;_____ in tu - o ad -
pa - ra - dise;_____ may saints in their

-ven - tu su - sci - pi - ant te mar - tyr - es,_____
glo - ry re - ceive your soul in pa - ra - dise,_____

49

12. Jesus Christ the Apple Tree

Words: from *Divine Hymns or Spiritual Songs*
New Hampshire, 1784

Music: Derek Holman

His beau-ty doth all things ex - cel: By faith_ I know, but ne'er can tell_____ The glo-ry which I now can see in Je - sus Christ the ap - ple tree.

For hap - pi - ness_ I_ long have sought,_

Ped.

And plea-sure dear-ly I have bought; _____ I _____

miss'd of _ all; _ but _ now I see 'Tis found in Christ the _ ap - ple tree.

Man.

I'm wea - ry with my

for - mer toil, Here will _ I sit and rest a - while: Un - der the

For the Boy Singers, Chiswick

13. Love Is Come Again

Words: Canon J. Crum*

Music: Bill Tamblyn

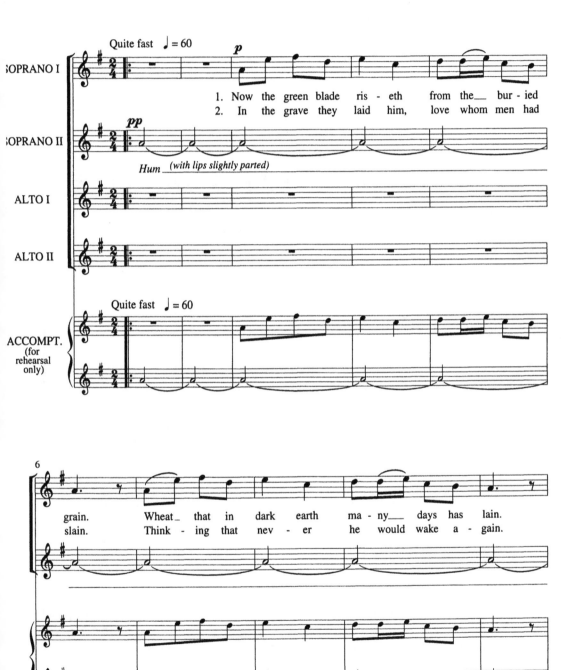

Love lives a - gain, that with the dead has been;
Laid in the earth like grain that sleeps un - seen;

Love is come a - gain like wheat that spring - eth green.
Love is come a - gain like wheat that spring - eth

green. 3. Forth he came at Eas - ter, like the ris - en grain.
3. Forth he came at Ea - ster, like the ris - en grain.

Lul lul lul lul lul lul lul lul lah
Lul lul lul lul lul lul lul lul lah

He_ that for three days in the_ grave had lain. Quick from the dead, my_

He_ that for three days in the_ grave had lain. Quick from the dead, my

ah_____ Quick from the dead, my

ah_____ Quick from the dead, my_

ris - en Lord is seen: Love comes like wheat that spring - eth green.__

ris - en Lord is seen: Love is come a - gain like wheat that spring - eth green.__

ris - en Lord is seen: Love is come a - gain like what that spring - eth green.__

ris - en Lord is seen: Love is come a - gain like_ wheat that spring - eth green.__

4. When our hearts are win - try, griev-ing_ or in pain,

Thy_ touch can call

4. When our hearts are win - try, griev-ing_ or in pain,_

Thy_ touch can

Fields of our hearts that dead and bare have

us back to_ life a - gain._

Fields of our hearts that dead and bare have been._

call us back to_ life a - gain.

been. Love is come a - gain like wheat that spring - eth green.

Love is come a - gain like wheat that spring - eth green.

Love is come a - gain like wheat that spring - eth green.

Love is come a - gain, like wheat that spring - eth green.

5. In the grave they laid him, love whom men had slain.

5. In the grave they laid him, love whom men had

5. In the grave they laid him, love whom men had slain.

5. In the grave they laid him, love whom

from the_ bur - ied grain. Wheat that in dark earth ma - ny_ days has

lain. Love lives a - gain, that with the dead has been; Love is come a -

- gain like wheat that_ spring - eth green.

Rall.

ALTO I
pp
Lul lul lul lul lul lul lul lul lah.

ALTO II
pp
Lul lul lul lul lul lul lul lul lah.

Rall.

For St Peter's Junior Choir

14. Make Me a Light

Words: Philip Wilby

Music: Philip Wilby

* Extra voices (ad lib.)   † Optional countermelody last (4th) time only.

© Copyright for all countries 1988 Chester Music Limited

4th time to CODA ⊕

1. 2. 3.

word, that I may shine with your love.

seen your sal - va - tion pre - pared for all peo - ple.

that I may shine with your love.

G[maj7]   Em   Am   D7   G   A   B7

VERSES

1. I hold a can - dle in my hands, Light which I
2. I hold a mir - ror in my hands, There what I
3. I hold a seed with - in my hands, Lend me your

p

E   A   B   E   C#m

hold and which I hold true, Light of the world shine
am and what I may do, Shines back to me in
help to make it grow Into the sweet scent - ed
In - to the sweet - est

Ah

F#m   G   E   E   A

66

35

out in the dark, May__ it al - ways re - mind me of
your glor - ious light, Make me a wor - thy re - flec - tion of
flow - er, That it may love - li - er flow - ers
scent - ed flow'r

*Ah*__

B   E   Am   D⁷   D

40

Repeat CHORUS

You._____
You._____
sow._____

Make me a

G   Am   G   C   C/D

44   ⊕ CODA

love._____

peo - ple._____

G   Am   G   C   Am⁷/D   G

D.G.F.A.

67

For St. Edmundsbury Cathedral Girls Choir in its tenth anniversary year

15. Mater Ora Filium

Words: 15th. century

Music: Charles Wood, arr. Harrison Oxley

save man - kind that was for - lorn. *Ma - ter o - ra fi - li - um,*

Ut post hoc ex - i - li - um _____ *No - bis do - net gau - di - um,*

Be - a - to - rum om - ni - um.

3. Three kings brought him pre - sents,__ Gold,__ myrrh, and frank - in - cense,

To my Son___ full of might,___ King of kings and lord of right.

Mater o - ra fi - li - um, Ut post hoc ex - i - li - um___

ah___ ah___

ah___ ah___

___No - bis do - net gau - di - um, Be - a - to - rum om - ni - um.

ah___

ah___

TWO or THREE VOICES

mp hum with lips slightly apart

er_____ er_____

f FULL

4. Fair mai - den, pray for us un - to thy Son, sweet Je - sus, That

mf legato

er_____ er_____

he will send us of his grace In heav'n on high to have a place.

mf SOLO I

Ma - ter o - ra fi - li - um, Ut post hoc ex - i - li - um

I *p*

ah_____ ah_____

II *p*

ah_____ ah_____

p

Man.

16. My Song Is Love Unknown

Words: Samuel Crossman

Music: Malcolm Archer

For Simon McGregor and the Choir of Westminster Under School, London

17. O for a Closer Walk with God

Words: William Cowper

Music: Anthony Cæsar

1. O for a closer walk with God, A calm and heavenly frame; A light to shine upon the road that leads me to the Lamb!

To Pepe and Barton

18. O Hear Us, Lord

Words: John Donne

Music: Anthony Piccolo

* small notes: alternative, only if necessary

9 November 1973

For the boys of Ampleforth

19. O Sacrum Convivium

Words: St Thomas Aquinas (attrib.)

Music: Kenneth Leighton

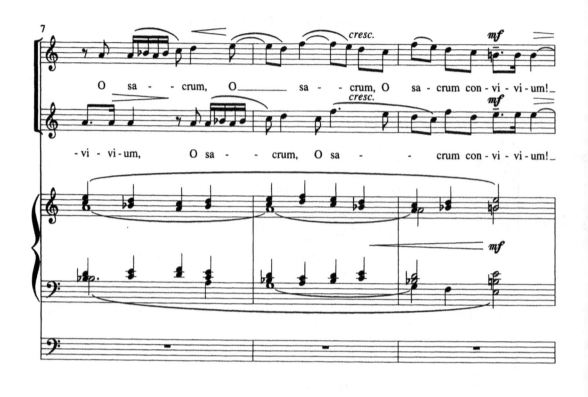

cresc. f *più intenso*

Chris - - tus su - mi - tur: re - co - li - tur___ me - mo - ri - a___ pas - -

cresc. f *più intenso*

Chris - - tus su - mi - tur: re - co - li - tur___ me - mo - ri - a___ pas -

più f legato

- -si - o - nis e - jus mens_____ im - ple - tur

- - -si - o - nis e - jus mens_____

gra - ti - a: et fu - tu - rae___

___ im - ple - tur gra - ti - a: et___ fu - tu - rae___

cresc.

glo - ri - ae,___ glo - ri - ae no -

glo - ri - ae,___ glo - ri - ae no - bis,

f

- -ia,_____ Al - le - lu - - - ia, Al - le - lu -

-lu - - ia,_____ Al - le - lu - - - ia, Al - le -

___ Al - le - lu - - ia,_____ Al - le - lu - - ia,_____ Al - le - lu -

- - ia._____

-lu - - ia,_____ Al - le - lu - ia,_____ Al - le - lu - ia._____

- - ia,_____ Al - le - lu - ia, Al - le - lu - ia.

20. O Sing Unto The Lord

Words: from Psalm 149

Music: Noel Rawsthorne

* optional divisions for upper and lower voices.

name in the dance. Let them sing prais - es un - to Man.

him___ with tab - ret and harp. Let the

Saints be joy - ful in glo - ry.

O sing un - to the Lord a new song.___

Commissioned by Walthamstow Hall, Sevenoaks, for Miss Elfreda Davies
on the occasion of her retirement, 12 November 1983.

21. A Song of St Francis

Words: Attributed to St Francis of Assissi

Music: Michael Hurd

to be un-der-stood, as to un-der-stand; to be loved, as to

love; for it is in giv-ing that we re-

22. What Songs Are These?

Words: Frank Kendon*

Music: Richard Lloyd

1. What songs are these, faint heard and far? The wind may be in

palm trees_ tall, Or runn - ing stream_____ or night - bird's_ call

the dark lies deep on des - ert, Where Jo - seph walk'd and

Ma - ry rode, the dark lies deep on des - ert:

Sleep well, thou child of God, sleep well, thou

child of God.

3. What forms are these, clear on the dark, that shine and yet are flesh and blood, that laugh and sing along the road, It is a crowd of child - ren, Where Jo - seph walk'd and Ma - ry rode, a

sing - ing crowd of_ child - ren — sleep well, thou

child of_ God, sleep well, thou child___ of_

God.

4. Ne - ver was seen so_ strange a_ guard, a - bout the

4. Ne - ver was seen so strange a guard, a - bout the foot - sore

Sleep well, thou child of__ God, sleep__

Sleep well, thou child of__ God, sleep

well, thou child_____ of__ God._____

well, thou child_____ of__ God._____

About the composers and the anthems

Biographical notes about the composers, and some information about the anthems, are given below. It is hoped that these will be of general interest, as well as providing material for programme notes and service sheets, if required.

Malcolm Archer was born in 1952. A prolific composer, he has more than 100 published works to his credit. He also has a demanding career as an organist that has taken him to Europe, Canada and the USA, and he has made many recordings, besides regular broadcasts for the BBC. The winner of an RCO scholarship to the Royal College of Music, he subsequently went up to Cambridge as Organ Scholar of Jesus College, and also became conductor of one of the University orchestras. He studied with Ralph Downes, Gillian Weir and Nicholas Kynaston. He then became Assistant Organist of Norwich Cathedral, moving in 1983 from there to the post of Organist and Master of the Choristers at Bristol Cathedral. Malcolm Archer is also the founder and Musical Director of the City of Bristol Choir and is currently Head of Chapel Music at Clifton College, Bristol.

My Song is Love Unknown was written for the Choristers of Bristol Cathedral, while Malcolm Archer was Organist and Master of the Choristers there. The words, familiar as a hymn text, were written by Samuel Crossman (1624–83), a former Dean of Bristol Cathedral whose tomb is in the south aisle.

Peter Aston was born in Birmingham in 1938, studied at the Birmingham School of Music and later, as a postgraduate, at the University of York. He also studied composition privately with Wilfrid Mellers. In 1964 he was appointed Lecturer in Music at York and he became Professor and Head of Music at the University of East Anglia in 1974. As a composer Aston's work has been mainly for voices, reflecting his activities as a conductor and the inspiration he finds in setting religious texts. Several of his anthems and services are firmly established in the cathedral choir repertoire, but he regards composing for less experienced singers as a no less important challenge. Much of his work is easily accessible to small amateur choirs, and is widely performed in churches throughout the world.

I give you a new commandment was written in 1994 in response to a request by the RSCM for a simple anthem for two voices, with accompaniment. The text was chosen by the composer, perhaps as a response to Tallis's famous anthem, *If ye love me*. The result is a beautiful setting that may be sung by any combination of voices, with organ or piano accompaniment.

Mark Blatchly was born in Shepton Mallet in Somerset in 1960. He was a chorister at Guildford Cathedral (1968–1973) under Barry Rose whom he later served as organ scholar at St Paul's Cathedral (1977–1978). From 1978 to 1981 he held an organ scholarship at Christ Church, Oxford under Simon Preston, before working as a freelance musician in London. In 1983 he was appointed Assistant Organist to John Sanders at Gloucester Cathedral and in 1990 became Organist of St Edmundsbury Cathedral. He left this post in 1992 to concentrate on composing, playing and teaching.

For the fallen was written for Barry Rose's choristers to sing at the Albert Hall Festival of Remembrance in 1980. The text is taken from Laurence Binyon's *For the Fallen* which was written in September 1914.

Anthony Cæsar was born in 1924. He was a chorister of Winchester Cathedral under Harold Rhodes, a music scholar of Cranleigh School and later of Magdalene College, Cambridge, where he was awarded the John Stewart of Rannoch scholarship in sacred music. Among his tutors were Hubert Middleton, Harold Darke and Patrick Hadley. He was assistant music master at Eton College under Sydney Watson and organist of Windsor Parish Church, before becoming Precentor (Director of Music) of Radley College. Since his ordination in 1961 his ministry has included being Chaplain of the RSCM, Precentor, Sacrist and Canon Residentiary of Winchester and Sub-Dean of HM Chapels Royal.

O for a closer walk with God was inspired by the singing of the boys of Westminster Under School while Simon McGregor, Sub-organist of the Chapel Royal, St James's Palace, was acting Director of Music.

Derek Holman was born in Redruth, Cornwall, in 1931. He was Tutor and later Warden of the RSCM from 1956 until he emigrated to Canada in 1965. He was organist of Grace Church-on-the-Hill, Toronto, from 1965 to 1979, and has been organist of St Simon's Anglican Church, Toronto, since 1981. Derek Holman is a prolific composer, and is a Professor of Theory and Composition at the University of Toronto.

Jesus Christ the apple tree was composed in 1971 at the request of Dr Gerald Knight, former Director of the RSCM. The text (after the allusion in the Song of Solomon 'As the apple tree among the trees in the wood, so is my beloved among the sons') has been traced back to a London magazine of 1761. It was included as an anonymous entry in Joshua Smith's collection *Divine Hymns or Spiritual Songs* published in New Hampshire in 1784, and this is now usually given as its source. The form of Holman's anthem is ABABA, and much of the musical material is derived from the triad D-B-G, which symbolises the 'apple tree'. Since its publication in 1971 by the RSCM the work has gained wide popularity in Britain and abroad.

Martin How was born in Liverpool in 1931. He was Music Scholar at Repton School and Organ Scholar at Clare College, Cambridge, graduating with a degree in music and theology. Apart from a short period as Organist at Grimsby Parish Church, Martin How has devoted most of his career to working for the RSCM and is acutely aware of the musical needs of choirs large and small.

An Easter Greeting typifies many of Martin How's works: scored for unison voices with divisions it may be sung with any combination of voices, men or women, by a group large or small. It is a triumphal setting of words adapted from a poem by Mrs C F Alexander and is ideal for Easter Day.

Michael Hurd was born in Gloucester in 1928 and read music at Pembroke College, Oxford, under Sir Thomas Armstrong and Dr Bernard Rose. He later studied composition with Sir Lennox Berkeley. In 1960, after six years on the staff of the Royal Marines School of Music, he settled in Hampshire where he has since worked as a freelance composer and author. His music includes opera, choral, orchestral, and chamber works. His many 'pop' cantatas, beginning in 1966 with *Jonah-man Jazz,* enjoy a worldwide popularity. As an author he has written many books including biographies of Ivor Gurney and Rutland Boughton, *An Outline History of European Music,* and the new *Oxford Junior Companion to Music.*

A Song of St Francis was commissioned by the distinguished mezzo-soprano Margaret Lensky to mark the retirement of the Headmistress of Walthamstow Hall, Sevenoaks, Miss Elfreda Davies. The poem, from *Praying Together,* an anthology of prayers collected by Philip Caraman SJ, was a particular favourite of Miss Davies. The first performance was given on 12 November 1983.

Kenneth Leighton was born in Wakefield in 1929. He began composing while he was still at school though his early career at Queen's College, Oxford was devoted to the study of classics. Later, still at Oxford, he concentrated his studies on music. He was a pupil of Bernard Rose and was also encouraged by Gerald Finzi who conducted several of his early works. Later he studied with Petrassi in Rome. In 1968 he was appointed Lecturer in Music and Fellow of Worcester College, Oxford and in 1970 he was made Reid Professor of Music at Edinburgh University. He died in 1988.

O sacrum convivium was written for Ampleforth College in 1980. The text is attributed to St Thomas Aquinas (1226–1274) and is highly suitable as a communion anthem: O sacred banquet in which Christ is received, the memory of his passion recalled, the soul is filled with grace, and a pledge of future glory is given to us. Alleluia.

Simon Lindley was born in 1948. He was educated at Magdalen College School, Oxford and later at the Royal College of Music where he was a pupil of John Birch. Between 1972 and 1974 he was a member of the RSCM's instrumental teaching staff at Addington and held posts in London and at St Albans before moving to Yorkshire in 1975. He is now Master of the Music at Leeds Parish Church and Leeds City Organist, as well as being a much-travelled Special Commissioner of the RSCM. Simon Lindley has produced many compositions and arrangements including several pieces for upper voices that have achieved widespread acceptance among choirs of all kinds.

Ave Maria is a litany to Mary with words taken from the *Angelus:* Hail, Mary, full of grace, the Lord is with thee, and blessed is the fruit of the womb, Jesus. Holy Mother, Mother of God, pray for us sinners now and at the hour of our death. Amen. The work was composed for use at services sung by the Boys' Voices alone at Leeds Parish Church, and was first sung there in March 1979. Although there is some vocal division in the second section, and at the final cadence, the piece may also be sung as a solo or as a duet.

Richard Lloyd was born near Manchester in 1933. He was a chorister in Lichfield Cathedral and studied at Rugby and Cambridge. During National Service he qualified in clerical skills and as a tank gunner, as well as being a choirmaster and compiler of a guide to Paris restaurants! He then spent some years as Assistant Organist at Salisbury Cathedral. In 1966 he became Organist of Hereford Cathedral, and moved to Durham in 1974, before returning to Salisbury to teach in the Cathedral School. He now devotes time to responding to commissions for church music, and following the cricket.

What songs are these? was written in December 1980 as a Christmas present for the composer's four daughters: Emma, Julia, Catharine and Olivia. It was first performed in Durham Cathedral by the cathedral choristers.

Simon Lole was born in 1957 and started his musical education as a chorister at St Paul's Cathedral. After reading for a music degree at King's College, University of London, and studying at the Guildhall School of Music, he returned to St Paul's Cathedral as Organ Scholar. In 1980 he was appointed Organist and Master of the Choristers at Croydon Parish Church and in 1985 moved to be full-time Director of Music for the parish of Warwick. He is now Master of the Music at Sheffield Cathedral.

The Father's Love was written in 1983 for a friend's wedding in Croydon Parish Church and was first performed by the Croindene Girls' Choir. The text, from John 15:9–12, is taken from the Jerusalem Bible.

William Mathias was born in Dyfed in 1934 and educated at Whitland Grammar School and at University College of Wales, Aberystwyth, where he studied with Ian Parrott. In 1956 he won an open scholarship in composition which took him to the Royal Academy of Music. From 1959 until 1968 he taught at University College, Bangor. He was elected a Fellow of the Royal Academy of Music in 1965 and in the following year received the DMus. from the University of Wales. Thereafter he also won several international awards. For a short time he held a lecturing post at Edinburgh University before returning to Wales and becoming Professor of Music at Bangor. His contribution to the organ music repertoire is highly significant and his church music and carols are regularly performed worldwide. William Mathias died in 1992.

Angelus, for SSA voices and piano, was completed on 9 September 1983 and given its first performance in 1984 by The Sirenian Singers, conducted by Jean Stanley-Jones. The composer uses words selected from the *Angelus,* with the following translation: The Angel of the Lord announced unto Mary. And she conceived of the Holy Ghost. Hail, Mary, full of grace, the Lord is with thee; blessed art thou among women, and blessed is the fruit of thy womb, Jesus. Behold the handmaid of the Lord. Be it done unto me according to thy word. Hail, Mary, full of grace, . . . And the word was made flesh and dwelt among us. Hail, Mary, full of grace,.. Pray for us, O Holy Mother of God. That we may be made worthy of the promises of Christ. Amen.

Colin Mawby was born in 1936. He was for many years Master of Music at Westminster Cathedral and is currently Choral Director for Radio Telefis Eireann—the Irish National Broadcasting and Television Company. His music is widely published and is popular in many countries.

I will lift up mine eyes, a setting of Psalm 121, taken from the Authorised Version of the Bible, was written for the wedding of a friend.

Harrison Oxley was born in 1933. As Organist of St Edmundsbury Cathedral in Suffolk from 1958 until 1984, Harrison Oxley was the pioneer in introducing girls' voices into English cathedral music. He is also widely known as an organ recitalist, festival adjudicator, examiner and composer, and since 1958 has been conductor of the St Edmundsbury Bach Choir and Orchestra.

Mater Ora Filium was dedicated to St Edmundsbury Cathedral Girls' Choir on its tenth anniversary in 1970. This publication in *The English Anthem Collection* coincides with another tenth anniversary: Harrison Oxley's present girls' choir specialising in cathedral music, the St Cecilia Singers, was founded in 1985.

Anthony Piccolo was born in New Jersey in 1946. Though not himself English, he has spent a number of years studying and working in England and has made a substantial and important contribution to the modern British choral repertory. Piccolo's earliest musical education began with piano lessons from the age of seven, followed by oboe, cello, viola, and singing lessons. He also made his first attempts at composition at the early age of eight. He obtained his degrees at the Peabody Conservatory of Music in Baltimore, Maryland, before going to the Guildhall School of Music in London where he obtained his Certificate of Advanced Studies. Between 1975 and 1984 he sang in the choirs of Lichfield Cathedral, Canterbury Cathedral and St Paul's Cathedral . He has since moved back to the United States of America and is currently Assistant Chorus Master at New York City Opera and Assistant Conductor of New Orleans Opera.

O hear us, Lord is one of Piccolo's earliest surviving compositions. It was written at a time when the composer had had very little exposure to the Anglican cathedral choral tradition. The inspiration for the work came from a long conversation with the dedicatees, who were cathedral choristers at the time, about the nature of their busy lives. The work has had at least four commercial recordings, by the Cathedral Choirs of Chester, Denver, the combined choirs of Washington and San Francisco, and Canterbury.

Noel Rawsthorne was born in Birkenhead in 1924 and began his musical career as a chorister at Liverpool Cathedral. In 1949 he was appointed Assistant Organist to Dr Harry Goss Custard at Liverpool. When Goss Custard retired in 1955, Rawsthorne succeeded him as Cathedral Organist, at the age of 25. He held this post with distinction for twenty-five years and in 1980 the Dean and Chapter conferred on him the honorary title of Organist Emeritus. From 1980 until 1984 Rawsthorne was City Organist at St George's Hall, Liverpool, which is home to a fine 1856 Father Willis organ. In 1993 he retired from his post of Senior Lecturer in Music at St Katharine's College in Liverpool after thirty-nine years in education, and in July 1994 the University of Liverpool conferred on him the degree of Doctor of Music *honoris causa.* As an organist Noel Rawsthorne has made many recordings with EMI and has recorded the Saint-Saëns Organ Symphony with both the Royal Liverpool Philharmonic Orchestra and the London Philharmonic Orchestra.

O Sing Unto the Lord was first published in 1993. A setting of Psalm 149, verses 1–5, it is composed in the style of a fanfare and is well-suited to festive occasions.

John Rutter was born in London in 1945. He was a chorister at Highgate School and went on to study music at Clare College, Cambridge, later becoming Director of Music there. In 1979 he gave up this post to concentrate on composing and conducting. Rutter also formed the Cambridge Singers at about this time, a professional chamber choir dedicated to recording his own, and other, choral music. He is in continuing demand as a guest conductor and lecturer and his work has a particular following in the United States of America.

A Gaelic Blessing, written for Mel Olson, was first published (scored for SATB choir and organ) by the RSCM in 1978. Since then it has gained wide popularity and in 1994 the composer produced two new arrangements of the work, for solo voice, and for SSA voices. The SSA arrangement is included in this collection with a piano accompaniment. However, the SATB version contains an organ arrangement of the accompaniment that may be used instead.

William Tamblyn was born in Birmingham in 1941. Since 1977 he has been Head of Music at Colchester Institute, where he leads study in Christian Liturgical Music. He is also a founder member of the St Thomas More Group. His music is widely published and recorded in Britain and USA.

Love is come again was prepared for a Musical Times supplement and is an arrangement of an accompanied SATB piece. The delightful text, based on John 12:24, was written for inclusion in the *Oxford Book of Carols* in 1928 by J M C Crum. The old French tune was, until Crum's words, associated with the Christmas carol *Noël nouvelet.*

Philip Wilby was born in Pontefract in 1949. He was educated at Leeds Grammar School and at Keble College, Oxford. He attributes his early interest in composition to Herbert Howells, whose extra-curricular composition classes he attended while a violinist in the National Youth Orchestra. He continued to compose during a period as a violinist with the Covent Garden Orchestra and the City of Birmingham Symphony Orchestra and in 1972 he was invited by Alexander Goehr to become Senior Lecturer in charge of Composition Studies at Leeds University, a post he still holds. He has written for both voices and instruments and has received numerous commissions from choirs and orchestras including two symphonies for the BBC Philharmonic Orchestra.

Make me a Light was written in 1984 for the Junior Choir at St Peter's Church in Harrogate where Wilby is Director of Music, at a time when his children were in the choir. Both practical and full of expressive qualities, it is written in an instantly attractive style.

Jonathan Willcocks was born in Worcester in 1953. He was a chorister at King's College, Cambridge and later became a Choral Scholar at Trinity College, Cambridge, taking an Honours degree in music. He now combines a career as a composer and conductor, working in Britain and abroad, with the role of Director of the Junior Academy, Royal Academy of Music, in London.

In paradisum was written in 1987 on the death of the composer's father-in-law, Philip MacNamara, and was first performed at his cremation service. The Latin text is taken from the Requiem Mass. The accompaniment is suitable for playing on either the piano or the organ.

Arthur Wills was born in Coventry in 1926. From 1958 until 1990 he was Director of Music at Ely Cathedral, and held a Professorship at the Royal Academy in London from 1964 to 1992. Dr Wills has toured extensively as a recitalist in Europe, the United States, Australia and Hong Kong, and has broadcast, appeared on television and made many recordings both as an organist and as Director of Ely Cathedral Choir. His secular music includes seven song cycles, and an opera 1984, based on the Orwell novel. He has composed prolifically for the organ, and his ensemble works include a Concerto with Strings and Timpani, a concerto for Guitar and Organ, and a symphonic suite called *The Fenlands* for Brass Band and Organ. His choral concerto *The Gods of Music,* which contains an important solo organ part, was premiered at the Newcastle Conservatorium in New South Wales, Australia, in 1992. His book *Organ* appeared in the Menuhin Music Guide Series in 1984, with a second edition in 1992. He was appointed OBE in 1990.

Ave Verum Corpus, together with O *Quam Gloriosum,* was first published as the first of *Two Latin Motets* by Novello and Company in 1960. It is dedicated to the Choristers of Ely Cathedral and was written for use at the early morning Eucharist services on Feast Days (services that were normally allotted to Boy's Voices alone then). Although written fairly early on in the composer's career, *Ave Verum* exhibits the mingling of modalism and chromaticism characteristic of his later work. The text may be interpreted thus: Jesus, Lamb of God, Redeemer, born the Virgin Mary's son: who upon the Cross a victim, has man's salvation won. From whose side, which man had pierced, flowed the water and the blood. By thy sacred body broken, be in life and death, our food.

Peter J Witchell was born in Bickley, Kent, in 1945. He was educated at Oxford University and the Royal Academy of Music and has a wealth of compositions to his credit, ranging from solo items through choral and orchestral works to pieces for music theatre. He has written incidental film music for the Video Unit of Leicester University, and his fourth musical, *Showhome*—written with Central Television writer Bob Hescott— was premiered in 1993. Recent compositions include a *Horn Concerto* (1992), and an *Oboe Concerto* for first performance in 1995. A regular conductor of choral and orchestral concerts, he is currently Director of Music at Oakham School, where he teaches composition and piano.

Fill thou my life was written for Augusta Miller, in response to a request for a short introit for her choir at Sherborne School for Girls. The words, by Horatius Bonar (1808–1889) are to be found in many hymn books, often to the tune *Richmond.*

Lightning Source UK Ltd.
Milton Keynes UK
UKOW05f1658140815

256946UK00001B/4/P